EVANGELICALS,

CATHOLICS

AND

UNITY

TODAY'S
ISSUES

EVANGELICALS,

CATHOLICS

AND

UNITY

MICHAEL
SCOTT
HORTON

CROSSWAY BOOKS • WHEATON, ILLINOIS
A DIVISION OF GOOD NEWS PUBLISHERS

Evangelicals, Catholics and Unity

Copyright © 1999 by the Alliance of Confessing Evangelicals

Published by Crossway Books
        a division of Good News Publishers
        1300 Crescent Street
        Wheaton, Illinois 60187

First printing, 1999

Printed in the United States of America

The Alliance of Confessing Evangelicals exists to call the church, amidst our dying culture, to repent of its worldliness, to recover and confess the truth of God's Word as did the Reformers, and to see that truth embodied in doctrine, worship and life.

Library of Congress Cataloging-in-Publication Data
Horton, Michael Scott.
    Evangelicals, catholics and unity / Michael Scott Horton.
    p.   cm. — (Today's issues)
    Includes bibliographical references.
    ISBN 1-58134-069-9 (booklet)
    1. Evangelicalism—Relations—Catholic Church. 2. Catholic
Church—Relations—Evangelicalism. 3. Evangelicalism and Christian
union. 4. Christian union—Catholic Church.   I. Title.
BR1641.C37H67   1999
280'.042—dc21   99-11516
                                       CIP

15	14	13	12	11	10	09	08	07	06	05	04	03	02	01
20	19	18	17	16	15	14	13	12	11	10	9	8	7	6	5	4	3

CONTENTS

Preface   7

1   Why Are We Still Divided?   9

2   Are Evangelicals Catholic?   13

3   Are Catholics Evangelical?   17

4   Two Obstacles to Unity   21

5   A Further Obstacle to Unity   31

6   Two More Obstacles to Unity   39

Conclusion   43

For Further Reading   48

PREFACE

These are not good days for the evangelical church, and anyone who steps back from what is going on for a moment to try to evaluate our life and times will understand that.

In the last few years a number of important books have been published all trying to understand what is happening, and they are saying much the same thing even though the authors come from fairly different backgrounds and are doing different work. One is by David F. Wells, a theology professor at Gordon-Conwell Theological Seminary in Massachusetts. It is called *No Place for Truth*. A second is by Michael Scott Horton, vice president of the Alliance of Confessing Evangelicals. His book is called *Power Religion*. The third is by the well-known pastor of Grace Community Church in California, John F. MacArthur. It is called *Ashamed of the Gospel*. Each of these authors is writing about the evangelical church, not the liberal church, and a person can get an idea of what each is saying from the titles alone.

Yet the subtitles are even more revealing. The subtitle of Wells's book reads *Or Whatever Happened to Evangelical Theology?* The subtitle of Horton's book is *The Selling Out of the Evangelical Church*. The subtitle of John MacArthur's work proclaims, *When the Church Becomes Like the World*.

When you put these together, you realize that these careful observers of the current church scene perceive that today evangelicalism is seriously off base because it has abandoned its evangelical truth-heritage. The thesis of David Wells's book is that the evangelical church is either dead or dying as a significant religious force because it has forgotten what it stands for. Instead of trying to do God's work in God's way, it is trying to build a prosperous earthly kingdom with secular tools. Thus, in spite of our apparent success we have been "living in a fool's paradise," Wells declared in an address to the National Association of Evangelicals in 1995.

John H. Armstrong, a founding member of the Alliance of Confessing Evangelicals, has edited a volume titled *The Coming Evangelical Crisis*. When he was asked not long afterwards whether he thought the crisis was still coming or is actually here, he admitted that in his judgment the crisis is already upon us.

The Alliance of Confessing Evangelicals is addressing this problem through seminars and conferences, radio programs, *modern* REFORMA-TION magazine, Reformation Societies, and scholarly writings. The series of booklets on today's issues is a further effort along these same lines. If you are troubled by the state of today's church and are helped by these booklets, we invite you to contact the Alliance at 1716 Spruce Street, Philadelphia, PA 19103. You can also phone us at 215-546-3696 or visit the Alliance at our website: www.AllianceNet.org. We would like to work with you under God "for a modern Reformation."

James Montgomery Boice
President, Alliance of Confessing Evangelicals
Series Editor

ONE

Why Are We Still Divided?

How can the church be the symphony of redemption when its musicians interpret the composition so differently that it sounds more like a wild cacophony than a harmonious concert?

The world wonders.

And so do we.

When we look in the Yellow Pages of the phone book for a certain church or a certain kind of church, we find a bewildering array of denominations. There are hundreds of denominations in America. In some regions, such as Northern Ireland and Central America, Protestants and Roman Catholics still even take up arms against each other. This is not only a scandal to the watching world; it is sometimes overwhelming, especially to new Christians who are simply seeking a solid nursery for their budding faith.

Meanwhile, the growing secularism of our time, reflected in the "culture of death" that naturalism, pragmatism, and relativism have unleashed, reduces the influence of religion in society nearly to the vanishing point. In such an environment, when committed Roman Catholics and Protestants share so much in common, highlighting remaining doctrinal differences strikes many persons as foolishly fiddling while Rome burns.

It is no wonder, then, that there is strong impatience with the divisions that haunt Christian witness at the end of its second millennium. Billy Graham's crusades broke with a fundamentalism that tended to identify Roman Catholicism with everything that is wrong in the world. Graham has even included local priests and distinguished Roman Catholic leaders on his crusade platforms. Pope John XXIII and the Second Vatican Council opened the windows and allowed the breezes of Eastern Orthodoxy and Protestantism (both liberal and evangelical) to blow through Rome's hallowed halls. Modernity, against which Rome had struggled more valiantly in many respects than mainline Protestants, was at last allowed entry, and many changes followed—at least on the surface. Especially in the United States, Protestants and Roman Catholics began to intermarry as religious differences, if not religion itself, receded in importance. There have been countless dialogues, some of them quite helpful in reaching greater understanding of both differences and agreements.

The charismatic movement, Bible study groups, Promise Keepers, the pro-life movement, and other grassroots efforts have drawn individual members of both communions together in non-ecclesiastical ways despite the official church divisions. All of us have come face to face with strangers and have often found them to be friends. In fact, in many cases we have found them to be true brothers and sisters in Christ.

So it happened that in 1994 and 1997, when a group of evangelicals and Roman Catholics drew up two bases of agreement ("Evangelicals and Catholics Together" and "The Gift of Salvation"), many took this as a sign that the issues that have separated the two communions for nearly five centuries were no longer obstacles to genuine unity and fellowship in a shared understanding of the Gospel.

All this has been confusing and troubling for many believers who sincerely long for greater visible unity among Christ's flock. We wish for unity but cannot willingly surrender essential truth in order to accomplish a false peace. For those who care about such truth, Christian unity must be a marriage made in heaven, not a merger or acquisition made on earth. Yet we ask: How should we navigate these troubled waters?

Let's begin by asking two important questions. First, are evangelicals catholic? Second, may Roman Catholics be considered evangelical?

TWO

Are Evangelicals Catholic?

In the churches of the Protestant Reformation, the Apostles' or Nicene Creed is recited regularly, including the line, "I believe in one holy, catholic, and apostolic church." *Catholic* means universal, and it refers to those truths that are, as St. Paul identified them, to be held "without controversy" (1 Tim. 3:16, KJV). It also refers to that body of Christians who, distinct from the heretical and schismatic sects that have plagued Christian unity throughout the ages, submit to the doctrine and discipline of Christ as he mediates his prophetic, priestly, and kingly ministry in the visible church through the Scriptures.

Unfortunately, the impression is sometimes given in Protestant circles that the Christian church started with Billy Graham or with the Reformation, while in fact the Reformation was an attempt to recover the ancient faith from the excesses of human pride and folly that had occurred in the Middle Ages. The Reformers were not trying to start a new church. That is why the Reformation was called the Reformation and not the Revolution. Martin Luther, John Calvin, and the other Reformers saw themselves not as new apostles or prophets sent to establish a new and higher kingdom, but as ministers of the "one holy, catholic, and apostolic church" that had existed by God's grace throughout the ages. They identified themselves with this "one holy, catholic, and apostolic church." And we do also.

It was the early Roman Catholic Church that successfully opposed the Gnostics, Arians, Pelagians, and numerous other false movements, and we who count ourselves evangelical Protestants belong to this Catholic Church today, a church founded by Christ on the ministry of the prophets and apostles. Unfortunately, in the Middle Ages especially, the western branch of this Catholic Church (which had already divided into an East-West schism) became increasingly corrupt. In the eleventh century there were as many as three rival popes, each declaring the others false popes and their realms of ecclesiastical jurisdiction anathema. Superstition, ignorance, the Crusades, the Inquisition, and an ambitious and self-indulgent papacy are all very well-known, and Rome has been more than willing to acknowledge many of these sins publicly in recent years.

But this is not why the Reformation happened. Savonarola, Erasmus, and others had touched on these problems and had urged greater morality and genuine piety, excoriating church corruption. Reform movements had called upon the church to improve the role of the laity. Many lay movements were founded to promote deeper and more genuine zeal. But Luther's concerns differed from these other attempts at reform. Luther dared to challenge medieval doctrine that had corrupted the ancient faith, and also the prevailing blind trust that most people had placed in the authority of popes and councils. Luther did this because he saw that the church needed more than mere renewal or an effective public relations campaign. It needed the Gospel. The Gospel was the source of its life, and its absence was its tomb. Still, the Reformers were staunchly opposed to the idea of sweeping away the visible church of their century and starting over. That notion was left to the radical sects. Like Luther, Calvin also emphasized reform rather than revolution.

Catholic in the best sense of the word, the Reformers overwhelmed their opponents with citations from the Church Fathers as well as from Scripture. In fact, they burned the midnight oil to preserve the bond of unity, meeting with Roman Catholic officials wherever and whenever they were invited. There was still hope that at last light would dawn, the more biblically literate among the cardinals would prevail, and an ecumenical council would finally resolve the conflict in favor of the Gospel as it is summarized in the formula, "by grace alone, through faith alone, because of Christ alone."

It was a papacy drunk with its own tyrannical power and ambition that sundered the unity of the western church, just as it had in its schism with the East in A.D. 1054. Whether Rome became schismatic rather than catholic is an open question, but whatever the case with Rome, it is undeniable that the leaders of the Reformation were catholic in the best sense of that word.

THREE

Are Catholics Evangelical?

To be *Catholic*, at least according to the ancient church and both the Orthodox and Protestant traditions, one does not have to belong to the Roman Catholic communion. It is, not surprisingly, only the Roman Catholic Church as it has existed since the Reformation that demands obedience to its sole primacy as the fundamental requirement for catholicity. Of course, this is itself a perpetual act of schism, for a church that places itself over all others has seriously compromised its claim to being catholic.

It is not strange that evangelicals should consider themselves catholic, as the Reformers themselves did. What is surprising is that a growing number of today's Roman Catholics refer to themselves as evangelicals. Keith A. Fournier asks whether "evangelical Catholic" is a "contradiction in terms" and answers his question in the negative (*Evangelical Catholics: A Call for Christian Cooperation*). What has happened to make this strange shift possible? Has Rome changed its answer to the question so critical to the Reformers, namely, "How are we saved?" Not at all, as one may discern from the new Catholic Catechism. After all, the Council of Trent (1545-1563) declared evangelicals to be "anathema," and according to Roman Catholic teaching itself, Rome's teaching cannot change. The

Latin phrase for this is *semper idem*. If a Roman Catholic can call himself an "evangelical," only two options present themselves:

> 1. Either that person is not loyal to the infallibly binding dogma of Rome, or
>
> 2. He or she does not mean by *evangelical* what those condemned by the Council of Trent intended when they identified themselves as evangelicals and were recognized as evangelicals by Trent.

Keith Fournier gives us a clue as to which course he takes when he turns to the *Westminster Dictionary of Christian Spirituality* for his definition of *evangelical*. This definition focuses entirely on piety rather than on doctrine. Included in the description is regular daily Bible study, prayer, devotions, diaries for intense self-examination, and so forth. The dictionary article on "evangelical" notes that these practices are "the evangelical equivalent of the confessional." Thus Fournier understandably concludes, "I am that kind of Christian, and I hope to become even more so in the years I have left."

At this point, many evangelicals will be on their feet applauding, even though this is a confession of piety rather than a confession of faith. The reason for this is that many evangelicals are more comfortable with the former than the latter. Roman Catholics who talk about being born again, "living in the Spirit," and "living for Jesus" strike a familiar chord with evangelicals. But these terms do not represent the slightest change in Roman Catholic dogma. The difference between Rome and the Reformation was never over the reality of the new birth, sanctification, or good works. Instead, it had to do with Rome's confusion of these unquestionably good things with the Gospel of God's justifica-

tion of sinners by an alien or imputed righteousness, the righteousness of Jesus Christ alone, rather
than by anything in or produced in themselves.

To the extent that contemporary evangelicals
have exalted piety over doctrine, they have become
indistinguishable from pious Roman Catholics. So
it makes sense that Roman Catholics can consider
themselves evangelicals while retaining full alle-
giance to that body's erroneous but binding dogma.

Let's ask an important question: What if the
term *evangelical* is defined not by spirituality but by
doctrine? What if Keith Fournier had turned to the
Westminster Dictionary of Theology instead of the
Westminster Dictionary of Spirituality, for example?
The former reads, "Derived from *euangelion* (evan-
gel, gospel, good news), the term came into use at
the Reformation to identify Protestants, especially
as they held to the belief in justification by grace
through faith and the supreme authority of
Scripture (often considered the material and formal
principles of Reformation teaching)." Quite clearly,
a Roman Catholic could not be identified as an
evangelical according to this doctrinal definition.

In his foreword to Fournier's book, evangelical
leader Charles Colson writes, "If you are an orthodox Catholic, you may find you are truly part of the
evangelical camp." My heart, like the hearts of
many, wants to agree with Colson on this point. But
if his statement is true, *evangelical* will mean something very different from that clear theological definition we find in the *Westminster Dictionary of
Theology*. Actually, the only reason I can count many
Roman Catholics among my brothers and sisters in
Christ is precisely that I do not consider them
orthodox Roman Catholics. If they were, they
would consciously be denying articles that are
essential to the Gospel.

On the other hand, perhaps Mr. Colson is cor-
rect—not in terms of what *evangelical* has meant

historically, but in regard to what the word has come to mean now. Perhaps it is true that orthodox Roman Catholics may find that they are "truly part of the evangelical camp," especially given the fact that this camp is increasingly removed from its doctrinal substance. But if that is the case, it is not only proof of a sad decline in the meaning of the word *evangelical*, but an instructive example of an even more tragic theological decline among historic evangelicals themselves.

FOUR

Two Obstacles to Unity

The greatest hope we can have in this matter is that both Protestants and Roman Catholics will enter a new period of reformation and come out on the other end of it with genuine agreement in the Gospel. What stands in the way? Is it simple complacency? Mere nastiness? Theological provincialism? Perhaps an unwillingness to overcome our unjustified fears of change? To be sure, complacency stalks conservative churches. Suspicion of "outsiders" is the haven of small minds. But the obstacles are not merely temperamental or differences in personality types.

The Formal Principle of the Reformation

Because it is the thing that forms, shapes, and determines what we believe as Christians, the Reformers singled out Holy Scripture as the sole sufficient source for faith and practice. "Scripture alone" (*sola Scriptura*) was the phrase used, and it meant that the church could not preach, teach, command, or practice anything contrary to Scripture, even for good reasons. The church's only authority was its faithful interpretation and teaching of the Bible. Erroneous interpretations were not made legitimate by claims for a supposedly infallible teaching office.

This did not mean that each person became his or her own interpreter of Scripture, however, though this error has received widespread support in many Protestant bodies. Luther, in fact, said this would mean only that every person would go to hell in his own way. Scripture alone was to be the final court of appeal for truth and life, but Scripture was to be interpreted communally and not individually. For this reason, Reformation churches not only embraced the ecumenical creeds but carefully crafted confessions of faith and catechisms. The purposes of these instruments was to provide a clearly defined agreement on the major teachings of Scripture in order to engender unity in the truth, to hold ministers in check, and to instruct the young and new converts in the true faith.

John Calvin saw Rome and the radical sects as ironically similar in one important respect: both failed to regard the Word as sufficient since both made their own claims to ongoing revelation. Calvin and the other Reformers taught that the Spirit rules neither through the tyranny of popes nor that of self-appointed prophets. Nor is this a free-for-all in which individual Christians are released from obligation to the official teaching and instruction of those officers whom God has placed in authority over them.

At the heart of this formal principle was the perspicuity or clarity of Scripture. Obviously, if the Bible is unclear, making it available to the laity would invite schism and heresy. The last two centuries of American Protestantism would confirm Rome's greatest fears in this respect. Still, the Reformers were convinced that the Bible *is* clear—that is, so long as teachers, pastors, and theologians are not busying themselves with turning the straightforward statements of Scripture into puzzles.

The Bible is not equally clear about everything, of course. It is clearer in declaring Christ's divinity than unfolding prophecy, for example.

Rome demands "implicit faith" (acceptance of

doctrinal teaching even apart from understanding) on the part of the faithful with respect to all the dogmas of the church. Protestants, however, distinguish between the chief articles that one must understand and personally embrace (for example, the articles of the Creed) and those that are important in lesser degrees.

How do we know what articles are essential? Again, the clarity of Scripture resolves this dilemma. The question that runs through the Bible from Genesis to Revelation is: How can we be reconciled to God? That was Israel's ancient longing as believing Jews looked to Christ through the shadows of the temple, sacrifices, priesthood, kings, and prophets, and it is the refrain of the New Testament too: "What must I do to be saved?" (Acts 16:30). This is answered so many times, so clearly, and its importance is ranked by Scripture itself so unambiguously that one can never conclude that the answer is insignificant or unclear. It is no mere fine point of theology, but the business upon which our eternal destiny depends.

Think of the apostle Paul's statement in Romans 10. Applauding his fellow-Israelites for their zeal, he nevertheless laments that theirs is a zeal "not based on knowledge." And this is not just knowledge in general, but knowledge of a particular truth: the doctrine of justification by grace alone through faith alone because of Christ alone. "Since they did not know the righteousness that comes from God and sought to establish their own, they did not submit to God's righteousness. Christ is the end of the law so that there may be righteousness for everyone who believes" (vv. 2-4). He could not be clearer. "All who rely on observing the law are under a curse" (Gal. 3:10). "To the man who does not work but trusts God who justifies the wicked, his faith is credited as righteousness" (Rom. 4:5). God designates as "blessed" those "to whom God credits righteousness apart from works" (Rom. 4:6).

Protestants, too, believe in the infallibility of tradition, if by that one is referring to the traditions of the apostles before they were committed to Scripture. Scripture refers to tradition. But it is called a *paratheke*, a given apostolic "deposit" (2 Tim. 1:14; 1 Tim. 6:20), not an evolving, post-apostolic, revelatory process. Thus the purpose of tradition after the apostles is not to reveal new truths, but to illumine, defend, and confess that which has already been revealed, which is why the early church councils appealed to the authority of Christ, the prophets, and the apostles rather than to their own authority as support for their statements.

It is no wonder that Rome teaches the dogma of "implicit faith." For how can an average layperson possibly hope to understand the hundreds of papal and conciliar declarations? One has to take the experts' word for it. But that is not how a good teacher teaches. Protestants argue that the Scriptures are so clear on the central points that if the church tells us otherwise, it is a poor teacher. A church that is a good teacher will, like our Lord himself with his disciples on the Emmaus road, open up the Scriptures to show us Christ on every page. For through the written Word we come into vital communion with the Living Word who has not left his children to be orphans.

The Material Principle

This leads us to the material principle of the Reformation, the second obstacle to visible unity with Rome—namely, the Gospel itself. If Scripture forms our faith and practice, the matter or content of the Gospel that it proclaims is nothing more nor less than Christ. Justification by grace alone through faith alone because of Christ alone! This is the material principle of Christianity, "the article by which the church stands or falls." At this point the difference between Protestant teaching and Roman Catholic teaching is insurmountable despite many sophisticated contemporary attempts to suggest that there really is no difference.

In the summer of 1998 it was reported that "more than 165 of Germany's top Protestant theologians . . . are criticizing a new Lutheran-Catholic statement that attempts to resolve historic differences on the doctrine of justification" (*Christianity Today*, June 16, 1998, p. 12). Objecting to the Lutheran World Federation's proposed agreement with the Vatican, these theologians—hardly what we would call conservatives— expressed surprise and outrage. Nobody wants the churches to remain divided. But as one German pastor put it, "What then is grace? What is faith? All of this remains unclear."

This is the heart of our concern too, for more important than being right in an argument is being right before God, and the issues that still divide Roman Catholics and evangelicals lead to two opposing ways of finding peace with God—that is to say, two different gospels.

Rome has never denied that grace is necessary for salvation, nor argued that one can be justified before God without faith. But, as with Scripture, neither grace nor faith are sufficient according to Roman Catholic dogma. In the fourth century the Catholic Church successfully resisted Pelagianism, the most common heresy of our sinful hearts. Pelagianism was essentially moralism. Sin was seen as the result of following Adam's poor example, and salvation was the result of following Christ's good example. Following Augustine's ambitious defense of the biblical message, the church condemned this form of blatant works-righteousness.

Nevertheless, Jerome's Latin Vulgate (Rome's official New Testament translation) was seriously flawed in a number of places and influenced the church for the worse. For instance, the Greek verb "to justify" (*dikaioō*), a courtroom term meaning "to declare righteous in the sight of the law," was translated by the Latin verb *justificare*, which meant "to make righteous." The difference is transparent and important. According to the former, an instant verdict is issued. According to the latter, something bad is gradually made good. In the Renaissance, humanists such as Erasmus pointed this out, and although they never actually joined the Reformation cause, their brilliant linguistic acumen cut a path for the Reformers.

Disagreement over the meaning of just this one verb ("to justify") is the sum and substance of the Reformation debate. It is the essence of what the whole conflagration was about. The question is simple: Is one declared righteous while still a sinner, as Paul said? Is it true that God "justifies the wicked" (Rom. 4:5)? Or is one declared righteous only after he or she has actually become righteous inherently? Luther held and all other genuine Protestants hold to the former.

But how can God declare me righteous if I am, in point of fact, unrighteous? Would this not make God a liar? Surely it would except for one fact: the perfect obedience of a person who was both God and man was imputed or credited to me as my righteousness before God's Law. In this understanding of salvation, the Law can only acquit me. No, more than that, it can only shower me with medals and announce to me that I am a legal heir of all Christ's riches, including adoption into the family of God. It is not that the Law is set aside, but that it is satisfied. Though we are still sinful, God takes delight in us because we are dressed in the perfect righteousness of his obedient Son.

This is the good news of Christianity. Without it, the news just isn't good news. "God justifies those who are doing their best to merit an increase in acceptance before God until finally they merit eternal life" is the gospel according to Rome, at least the one that is still binding on all loyal Roman Catholics. And that is not good news at all!

The Reformers wanted an ecumenical council that they believed might lead the church to affirm the true Gospel of justification by grace alone through faith alone because of Christ alone, but their efforts failed. The Council of Trent (1545-1563) was the official Roman Catholic response to the Reformation and its teachings. But sadly, it did not affirm the Gospel. The Council of Trent issued the following binding decrees on justification:

> Canon 9. If anyone says that the sinner is justified by faith alone, meaning that nothing else is required to cooperate in order to obtain the grace of justification . . . let him be anathema.
>
> Canon 11. If anyone says that men are justified either by the sole imputation of the righteousness of Christ or by the sole remission of sins, to the exclusion of the grace and charity which is poured forth in their hearts by the Holy Ghost (Rom. 5:5), and remains in them, or also that the grace by which we are justified is only the good will of God, let him be anathema.
>
> Canon 12. If anyone says that justifying faith is nothing else than confidence in divine mercy, which remits sins for Christ's sake, or that it is this confidence alone that justifies us, let him be anathema.
>
> Canon 24. If anyone says that the righteousness received is not preserved and also not increased before God through good works, but that those works are merely the fruits and signs of justification obtained,

but not the cause of the increase, let him be anathema.

Canon 30. If anyone says that after the reception of the grace of justification the guilt is so remitted and the debt of eternal punishment so blotted out to every repentant sinner, that no debt of temporal punishment remains to be discharged either in this world or in purgatory before the gates of heaven can be opened, let him be anathema.

Canon 32. If anyone says that the good works of the one justified are in such manner the gifts of God that they are not also the good merits of him justified; or that the one justified by the good works that he performs by the grace of God and the merit of Jesus Christ, whose living member he is, does not truly merit an increase of grace, eternal life, and in case he dies in grace the attainment of eternal life itself and also an increase of glory, let him be anathema.

These decrees affirm that men and women are accepted before God on the basis of their cooperation with God's grace over the course of their lives, rather than on the basis of the finished work of Christ alone, received through faith alone, to the glory of God alone. According to Roman Catholic teaching, justification (righteousness) is infused or poured into the infant born in original sin, making the child holy. This is purely an act of God's grace. But sins committed after baptism drain away some of this initial merit, and in the case of mortal sins a person is entirely emptied of this righteousness. For both mortal and venial sins, there are sacraments. For instance, in the sacrament of penance, which consists of contrition (feeling sorry for one's sins), confession, and satisfaction (making restitution), one may recover one's salvation. All grace after baptism is merited by the believer not because his acts are perfect, but because God accepts them as sufficient for the earning of eternal life.

This cheapens our understanding both of sin and salvation. As the eleventh-century thinker Anselm put it, "You have not yet considered how great your sins are." If God demands perfect righteousness, the good works that merit eternal life must not have even the slightest imperfection. So this righteousness must be the untarnished righteousness of Christ. And this is what we have! According to the Gospel, Christ's righteousness meets God's standard. Just as Adam's guilt was imputed to his posterity, rendering them unrighteous even apart from their first act of sin, so the Second Adam's righteousness is imputed to Christ's posterity, rendering them righteous even apart from their first act of obedience (Rom. 5:6-19).

What is it, then, that still keeps evangelicals and Roman Catholics apart?

Here is the answer: Scripture pronounces its anathema on any person or church that proclaims a false gospel of works-righteousness, and Rome is officially committed to such an erroneous gospel, not only at Trent but in its most recent Catholic Catechism. Thus while individual Roman Catholics may from ignorance or disobedience enter into the safety of the invisible and universal church of Christ, Rome itself cannot be considered a true visible church, for it has surrendered the most necessary mark of the true church, namely, the Gospel itself, by which alone we pass from spiritual death to new spiritual life.

FIVE

A Further Obstacle to Unity

The errors of Rome in regard to the authority of Scripture and the Gospel are not the only barriers to Evangelical and Roman Catholic unity, though they are the most serious. Other barriers include Roman Catholic claims to the supremacy of the pope, that church's Mariology, and its terrible teaching about purgatory. As far as the first claim goes, the recent Catholic Catechism statement is as clear as any: "The Roman Pontiff, by reason of his office as Vicar of Christ, and as pastor of the entire Church has full, supreme, and universal power over the whole Church, a power which he can always exercise unhindered."

Is the Pope the "Vicar of Christ on Earth," the "Holy Father" with whom all genuine Christians must be in communion if they wish to be received into full communion with Christ's body?

There are many reasons to reject such arrogance.

Papal Supremacy and Church Tradition

One of the attractive features of Rome, at a time when most Protestants do not seem to remember or care what happened last Tuesday, is that the Roman church has a long ecclesiastical tradition. Agree or disagree, Rome has stuck by her guns for a very long time. The Pharisees had a long and respected tradition too, of course, a tradition Jesus refuted. So argument by tradition does not in itself have unassailable credibility. But there is much more to be said in rejecting Rome's claim.

For one thing, Rome's appeal to tradition in support of papal supremacy is contradicted by much of that tradition. A host of ancient church fathers can be cited at this point. I will cite a few examples.

Cyprian (A.D. 200-258) declared, "Neither does any of us set himself up as a bishop of bishops, nor by tyrannical terror does any compel his colleague to the necessity of obedience; since every bishop, according to the allowance of his liberty and power, has his own proper right of judgment, and can no more be judged by another than he himself can judge another" (*Seventh Council of Carthage*, paragraph 1).

The Council of Nicea (A.D. 325) declared that each church center was to be ruled by its own bishop and not by one head over all bishops (Canon 6).

The Council of Chalcedon (A.D. 451) declared that Rome's rank was based on its political significance rather than any spiritual superiority (Canon 28).

Even Gregory I (A.D. 540-604), though himself bishop of Rome and interested in consolidating power under his jurisdiction, said of the word "universal" as it was being used to express an exaggerated claim to authority over others by the pontiff:

> None of my predecessors ever wished to use this profane word. For clearly if one patriarch is called "universal," then the name "patriarch" is taken away from the rest. . . . To consent to this wicked word is nothing less than to destroy the faith. . . . It is one thing that we should preserve unity

of faith; another, that we ought to repress self-exaltation. But I say it confidently, because whoever calls himself "universal bishop," or wishes to be so called, is in his self-exaltation Antichrist's precursor, for in his swaggering he sets himself before the rest. (*Epistle 18*)

What is the tradition then? Strikingly, the tradition of the ancient fathers of both the East and the West, even the bishop of Rome, is that the very doctrine of papal supremacy, which Rome eventually declared infallibly binding on all Christians, was at best an act of schism and disunity and at worst a claim worth comparing to the arch-usurper of Christ's authority, the Antichrist.

The Rise of Papal Claims

How then did the idea of papal supremacy and infallibility arise? Like most significant events in church history, there were many factors. But we may suggest a few.

1. *Rome was the center of the world.* Since Rome was the cultural, administrative, and political center of the West, it stood to reason that the Gentile missionary expansion would radiate from there. Although in the early centuries persecuted Christians saw Rome as the "City of Destruction," its "conversion" to Christianity under Constantine led many to revive the old pagan nickname and call Rome "the Eternal City," looking to it as the earthly focus of the church. By confusing God's kingdom with the agenda and prominence of their own secular kingdom, the Christians of Rome forgot that Christ's realm is ruled by grace, not glory. They forgot that we are called to suffering in this life prior to reigning in the next.

A growing popularity, including political favoritism, corrupted the church and transformed its missionary identity (the children in the wilderness ever on the march toward the promised land) into a self-centered and worldly passion for power, success, wealth, and prosperity here and now.

The Reformers protested against this corruption, seeking to restore both the liberty of Christians and godly order in the churches. All Christians are priests, they insisted, citing New Testament teaching; but not all priests are ministers. Paul told the Ephesians: "There is one body and one Spirit—just as you were called to one hope when you were called—one Lord, one faith, one baptism; one God and Father of all, who is over all and through all and in all" (Eph. 4:4-6). But this did not mean there were to be no authorities to whom Christians are accountable. Rather, Christ gave gifts so that some would be "apostles, some . . . prophets, some . . . evangelists, some . . . pastors and teachers" (verse 11), whose task was to promote solid maturity and the unity in the faith for which Jesus prayed in John 17.

When the apostolic ministry passed away, the offices of pastor and teacher continued, through which Jesus alone reigned as Lord, King, lawmaker, and revealer of all truth for his people. In asserting papal supremacy Rome not only rejected the consensus of the ancient church but Scripture, a clear instance of human pride undercutting true unity in the Spirit.

At the time of the Reformation Calvin asked: Since not even the apostles were free to roam beyond Scripture, why should popes, councils, and bishops claim the right to do it? Even Peter, supposedly the first pope, claimed nothing for himself or others except the duty of imparting the doctrines that had been handed down by God: "If anyone speaks, he should do it as one speaking the very words of God" (1 Pet. 4:11). In his *Institutes of the Christian Religion*, Calvin took his readers through a walking tour of church history, demonstrating by precise quotations from the fathers how Rome had broken the peace of Christ's church by its proud ambition for supremacy (book 4, chapters 6—8).

As the church grew increasingly worldly in its quest for power, so too did its ideas of leadership. Bishops began to don the regalia of secular rulers and saw themselves as princes of a sort. As a priest's counterpart was what we might call the mayor, the bishop's was the governor, and much of the elaborate dress that is worn today by Roman bishops is not apostolic or even distinctively religious, but was adopted from secular customs. This power grew during the Middle Ages, so that at last, according to Calvin, "the Roman pontiff, not content with modest baronies, first laid his hand upon kingdoms, then upon the Empire itself" (*Institutes*, book 11, chapter 11).

While the realities of a democratic age have significantly undercut Rome's traditional claims to even secular jurisdiction, the magisterium is as autocratic as ever with respect to its claim to sovereignty over souls. It is true that Protestants are recognized as "separated brothers." But so are adherents of other religions and even atheists who endeavor to be good people.

Rome has been utterly clear about this: full communion of Christians requires submission to the pope. "Unity" with Rome always implies movement away from one's own distinctives and absorption by Rome. It never means that two parties are reconciled in the truth, which neither body holds in perfect purity. According to the Roman Catholic doctrine of the church, unity always means that a Protestant moves closer to full communion with Christ's church only to the extent that he or she ceases to be a Protestant.

2. *Rome's spiritual leadership*. The Roman church obtained immense credibility throughout the Empire when Christianity was officially tolerated.

Furthermore, the first five centuries witnessed the greatest doctrinal crises in church history. In these debates the orthodox interpretations of such biblical doctrines as the Trinity, the two natures of Christ, original sin, and the need for grace were frequently defended by Rome. While other bishops were often less trustworthy in their interpretations of Scripture on these critical points, the bishops of Rome usually took the right stand when truth required resolute confidence. Thus the churches of Christ increasingly looked to the Roman bishop and his brother pastors for leadership and vision.

3. *The so-called "Donation of Constantine."* During the medieval period, Rome claimed that the pope was not only the lord of the church, but of the state as well, that he was sovereign over both kingdoms. This claim was opposed by many, of course. St. Bernard was one. He wrote that although the pope "claims this role for some other reason, yet it is not his by apostolic right. For Peter could not give what he did not have; but he gave to his successors what he had, the care of the churches" (cited by Calvin, *Institutes*, book 4, chapter 11, section 11).

Nevertheless, the popes defended this right on the basis of a document that Renaissance scholars later proved to be a fraud. Forged in the papal chambers under Pope Paul I (A.D. 757-767), the document purported to be a deed given by Constantine to Pope Silvester I, granting him secular control over much of the Empire, as if Constantine were bequeathing his power to the pope. The discovery of this forgery on the eve of the Reformation reminded many Protestants of the lengths to which Rome had been willing to go in its perverted ambition to rule the world rather than to minister to the faithful alongside the many other fellow-shepherds of the church under Christ, as she should have done.

Two Views of Unity

It is naive to think that the Second Vatican Council, the "modernizing" council of the 1960s, swept away these many centuries of papal claims to sovereignty. According to the Second Vatican Council, the pope is still "the visible source and foundation of the unity both of faith and of communion." The faithful must submit to the pope's words "even when he does not speak *ex cathedra*. . . ." His decisions "are rightly said to be irreformable by their very nature. . . ." They are even described as "revelation."

In its Decree on Ecumenism (*Unitatis Redintegratio*), the Council added that Protestants are still considered schismatics, since they have separated themselves from full communion with the church founded by Christ. Even though individual members of these bodies may be considered "brothers," these communions themselves must return to Rome and acknowledge its papal and conciliar pronouncements as binding if they are to be considered part of Christ's body:

> For it is through Christ's Catholic Church alone, which is the universal help towards salvation, that the fullness of the means of salvation can be obtained. It was to the apostolic college alone, of which Peter is the head, that we believe that Our Lord entrusted all the blessings of the New Covenant, in order to establish on earth the one Body of Christ into which all those should be fully incorporated who belong in any way to the people of God.

In Roman Catholic ecumenicism, the drive for unity is not considered a task requiring mutual understanding, recognition of faulty teaching, and hope for eventual reunion based on Scripture.

Rather, it is driven by the idea that to be truly Christian is to be Roman Catholic, and nothing short of becoming a Roman Catholic suffices for full communion with the body of Christ. Thus Protestants and Catholics can, by definition, never be in full communion, and it is naive, or perhaps ill-informed, to think that it can be any other way given the unyielding facts of Roman Catholic ecclesiology.

When the pope prays for unity, what he is asking is that Protestants will cease to be Protestants, that the "separated churches" will at last recognize their heresy and schism and return to submission to his authority. This is not because the pope is arrogant or crafty, but because the Roman doctrine of the church requires this position. That position has been stoutly defended by the magisterium up to the present hour.

North America has seen its share of home-grown Protestant cults and sects, each claiming to be the true church with the right leader who is in direct contact with God beyond his written Word. Although Rome's history of doing this sort of thing may be more ancient than those strangely American enclaves, it is essentially the same thing. Again, the Roman Catholic Church may have a stronger affinity with evangelical Christians on a number of important doctrines. But like all groups that claim a human authority beyond God's revealed Word, Rome's claims are riddled with historical inconsistencies, contradictions, and fabrications. These claims may comfort those seeking certainty in the midst of anxious times, but they are false bastions of security. They are castles built on sand.

SIX

Two More
Obstacles to Unity

The Reformers did not spend much time criticizing
Rome's devotion to Mary and the saints or purgatory because they knew that the real problem was
understanding how one is actually brought into a
saving relationship with God and not these deriva-
tive issues. If a person does not believe that Christ's
saving work is sufficient for salvation, it is quite
understandable that other mediators and other
works of merit than Christ's will be needed.

That is why these doctrines remain so strong in
the devotional life of modern Catholicism.
Evidently concluding that the intercession of Christ
is not sufficient for salvation, the decrees of the
Second Vatican Council encourage the cult of saints
and especially the cult of the Virgin and her intercession for sinners, her immaculate conception,
and her bodily assumption into heaven. "Therefore
the Blessed Virgin is invoked in the Church under
the titles of Advocate, Helper, Benefactress, and
Mediatrix." The faithful "turn their eyes to Mary,"
who "is the subject of preaching and worship." She
is "rightly honored by a special cult [worship] in
the Church."

One of the benefits of the new emphasis on
biblical studies among Roman Catholic scholars is
the candor with which many acknowledge that the
notion of purgatory has no basis in Scripture. This

does not require a break with official dogma, however (which would mean a break with Rome itself), because dogmas may be contained either in Scripture or in church tradition.

A discussion of the veneration of Mary and the saints goes hand in hand with a discussion of purgatory, as both have their source in the popular piety of those who were looking for role models and assistance from those who had suffered greatly for the faith and had gone on to their reward. Unlike the claims to papal supremacy, seeds of this notion were planted quite early in the church. It was forged in the furnace of persecution, where a theology of martyrdom evolved that glorified this ultimate sacrifice. Martyrs were immortalized in the early Christian memory as they stood in Roman forums to give up their lives for the life to come. Some Christians even actively sought martyrdom in the same manner in which, for instance, a Moslem would later sacrifice his life upon the promise of eternal salvation. A sort of merit system was operating, in practice if not always in theory.

Out of this experience, a theological rationale developed that not only held out special hopes for martyrs, but sought to explain how lapsed Christians could be restored to grace. Through all these practical pastoral problems, some influential churches in the ancient period moved increasingly away from the clear biblical proclamation of grace alone and borrowed on the old Adamic capital of self-help salvation.

An evangelical critique of purgatory hardly requires much space since, as even Roman Catholic theologians and exegetes concede, it is a doctrine that cannot be found either explicitly or implicitly in Scripture. It can hardly be an evangelical option.

But there is a further reason why a full study is rendered unnecessary. At the heart of the notion of purgatory is the idea of merit, and this is clearly at odds with everything that we have seen concerning the "chief article" of Christian doctrine: namely, we are justified or accepted before God by grace alone through faith alone on the sole basis of Christ's righteousness imputed to our account. The idea that one must spend an unknown period of time in purgatory, a place of suffering, in order to "work off" one's sins denies the finality and sufficiency of Christ's saving work. It comes under the anathema of St. Paul in Galatians. It is "a different gospel—which is really no gospel at all." It is not "good news" that after I die, I must be sent to purgatory—perhaps for a very long time—even though a perfect Substitute fully satisfied God's Law in my place and atoned for my sins. Nothing could be clearer than the fact that the doctrine of purgatory rests upon a false gospel of salvation by human works.

At the time of the Reformation, Pope Leo financed the building of Christendom's largest cathedral (St. Peter's in Rome) by selling indulgences. These notes, specifying release from a certain number of years in purgatory, could be purchased. And since the "Treasury of Merit," as it was called, was under the jurisdiction of the church, this merit could be dispensed (or sold) at the pope's discretion. It was this fund-raising tactic that raised Martin Luther's ire enough to cause him to draft his famous Ninety-Five Theses, which launched the Reformation. To this day visitors to some Roman Catholic cathedrals, especially in Italy, can view signs inviting the purchase of just such indulgences. An attempt to justify this practice is even explicitly and unabashedly made in the new Catholic Catechism. The good news of the Gospel, however, is that Christ has already paid the price for the full and free pardon of saved sinners.

Rome's repeated willingness to range beyond Scripture to invent new forms of church leadership, new means of redemption, and new sources of doctrine and worship disqualifies not only its haughty pretensions to universal supremacy, but even its claim to being a faithful witness to Jesus Christ in his saving mission to a lost and needy world.

The gospel of Rome is not the true biblical Gospel of salvation by grace alone through faith alone because of Christ alone, and no true Christian can knowingly join with such a false and spiritually tyrannical institution.

CONCLUSION

This is a very sad business, and difficult to argue. It is difficult for me because I have personal sympathies with so many Roman Catholic brothers and sisters. We share so much in common, and we are surrounded by myriad enemies. It is not surprising that the free fall of our culture should draw us toward the wider religious world, especially to those who take their religion seriously, as devout Catholics do. But Christianity does not preach a gospel of saving decadent cultures. It is not mere theism, philosophical apologetics, impressive cathedrals, and romantic myths of "Christendom." These mean next to nothing to true faith. At the end of the day Christianity is only itself—and therefore important and relevant—when it faithfully preaches the Gospel to the ends of the earth.

Speaking after the Second Vatican Council, Roman Catholic theologians may be far more irenic and conciliatory in their language with Protestants than many have been previously. But as Avery Dulles, S.J., a principal drafter of the "Evangelicals and Catholics Together" document, put it, "We were careful to follow Trent, the teaching of the Second Vatican Council. . . . We are not far-out Catholic theologians" (*Christianity Today*, April 27, 1998, p. 21).

In recent decades many Catholic theologians (especially New Testament scholars) have done much to promote understanding between the two traditions and in many cases have actually defended the evangelical interpretation of the most relevant passages. But the openness introduced by the Second Vatican Council has not addressed the condemnations of the Council of Trent. Recent pronouncements have lifted the excommunication placed on the Reformers, but not on their teaching. And this has fostered an environment that has opened the door for Protestant liberalism to invade Catholic ranks. While Trent at least defended the necessity of faith in Christ for salvation, Karl Rahner's notion of the "anonymous Christian," the idea that even an atheist may be saved as long as he or she is morally upstanding, became an actual dogma at the most recent council.

Since the Second Vatican Council many opportunities have been provided (and should be pursued) for dialogue. Nevertheless, the evangelical doctrine of justification is not merely a formulation of how one can *become* accepted before God; it is the announcement of how one *is* accepted before God. It is true that different Christian churches, given various national, historical, geographical, cultural-linguistic, and other considerations, will arrive at distinct formulations of the same truth. But when we come to the basic question "How am I saved?" there is no room for confusion or an agreement to disagree agreeably.

Rome answers that we are saved by grace plus works.

Genuinely apostolic churches answer with Paul, "But if it is by grace, then it is no longer by works; if it were, grace would no longer be grace" (Rom. 11:6).

Whether it is mainline Protestants involved with the recent accord between the World Lutheran Federation and the Vatican, or evangelicals claiming a common understanding of the Gospel that leaves the question of how one is justified open-ended, the biblical mandate for pursuing visible unity of the church presupposes unity in the

Gospel. And if the Gospel is still the message that God justifies the wicked, then that good news cannot be surrendered in order to build church unity on some other foundation.

There is no room for self-righteousness here. Rome has officially never tolerated the Pelagian heresy. Yet that seems to be the mark of most of American Protestantism with its optimistic view of human nature. Pollster George Barna reports that according to 77 percent of America's professing evangelicals, human beings are basically good, and 84 percent agree with the statement that in salvation, "God helps those who help themselves" (*What Americans Believe*, p. 89). Incredibly, the nineteenth-century revivalist Charles Finney, revered by many evangelicals, denied the doctrine of original sin and even the need for a substitutionary atonement, declaring that the doctrine "of justification by an imputed righteousness is [itself] another gospel" (*Systematic Theology*).

Today categories of sin and grace are often replaced with those of dysfunction and recovery. So we cannot criticize Rome while failing to point out the blatant Pelagianism of popular American religion. Even in conservative, evangelical churches, the clear note of justification is often missing. It is missing from the sermons, the liturgy, the singing, and the teaching. Even in churches that consider themselves heirs to the Protestant Reformation, trivial pursuits often push to the margins the proclamation of Christ in his saving office, from Genesis to Revelation.

So what is it that still keeps Roman Catholics and Protestants apart? Unless we define *evangelical* doctrinally, the answer is: absolutely nothing. If evangelicals no longer think evangelically, leaving the formal and material principles of the Reformation behind, there is nothing needed except paperwork to achieve unity. We can have an easy peace that costs nothing but the faithful confession of the Gospel in our particular time and place.

Instead of trying to forge false unity by weakening the only basis upon which true unity may be built, can we not establish church-sponsored forums in which greater understanding and cooperation may be fostered? In today's climate Protestantism, no less than Roman Catholicism, needs a new Reformation. Though we may not agree on the total package, mark the words of Roman Catholic theologian Johann Baptist Metz:

> To speak about the Reformation and make it, not just an object of remembrance, but an object of hope, indeed an incentive to change—change for all of us, including myself as a Catholic—means one thing: we must bring that question and that awareness which inspired the Reformation into a relationship with the present age. . . . Many theologians writing about the Reformation assure us nowadays that Luther's fundamental question regarding a gracious God can scarcely be made intelligible to people today, let alone communicated as relevant to their lives. This question is said to belong to another, non-contemporary world. I do not share this position at all. The heart of the Reformation's question—How can we attain to grace?—is absolutely central to our most pressing concerns. . . . The second Reformation concerns all Christians, is coming upon all of us, upon the two great churches of our Christianity. (*The Emergent Church*, pp. 48-50)

Is this beyond the sovereignty of God's Spirit to accomplish? With Christ we prayerfully answer, "With man this is impossible, but with God all things are possible" (Matt. 19:26). But until the official ban—not on individuals, but on the Gospel itself—is lifted by Rome, evangelicals must continue to witness faithfully to the exclusive claims of the church's only King by regarding these departures as fatal to any agreements that may be reached on important points. As we pray for unity and work for greater understanding, let us also not fail to "contend earnestly for the faith that was once for all entrusted to the saints" (Jude 4).

FOR FURTHER READING

Armstrong, John H. *A View of Rome: A Guide to Understanding the Beliefs and Practices of Roman Catholics.* Chicago: Moody Press, 1995.

Boice, James Montgomery. *Standing on the Rock: Biblical Authority in a Secular Age.* Grand Rapids: Baker, 1994.

— and Sasse, Benjamin E., editors. *Here We Stand: A Call from Confessing Evangelicals.* Grand Rapids: Baker, 1996.

Hodge, Charles. *Justification by Faith Alone.* Ed. John W. Robbins. Hobbs, N.M.: Trinity Foundation, 1995.

Kistler, Don and others. *Justification by Faith Alone: Affirming the Doctrine by Which the Church and the Individual Stands or Falls.* Morgan, Pa.: Soli Deo Gloria Publications, 1995.

Kistler, Don, editor. *Sola Scriptura: The Protestant Position on the Bible.* Morgan, Pa.: Soli Deo Gloria Publications, 1995.

McGrath, Alister E. *Justification by Faith: What It Means to Us Today.* Grand Rapids, Mich.: Zondervan, 1988.

Sproul, R. C. *Faith Alone: The Evangelical Doctrine of Justification.* Grand Rapids: Baker, 1995.

—. *Grace Unknown: The Heart of Reformed Theology.* Grand Rapids: Baker, 1997.

Webster, William. *The Gospel of the Reformation: Salvation from the Guilt and Power of Sin.* Battle Ground, Wash.: Christian Resources, 1997.

—. *Saving Faith: How Does Rome Define It?* Battle Ground, Wash.: Christian Resources, 1995.